HOW SOCCER WORKS

Keltie Thomas

Illustrations by Stephen MacEachern

MAPLE TREE PRESS

Maple Tree Press books are published by Owlkids Books Inc.
10 Lower Spadina Avenue, Suite 400, Toronto, Ontario M5V 2Z2 www.owlkids.com

Text © 2007 Keltie Thomas
Illustrations © 2007 Stephen MacEachern

Distributed in Canada by Raincoast Books
9050 Shaughnessy Street, Vancouver, British Columbia V6P 6E5

Distributed in the United States by Publishers Group West
1700 Fourth Street, Berkeley, California 94710

We acknowledge the financial support of the Canada Council for the Arts, the Ontario
Arts Council, the Government of Canada through the Book Publishing Industry
Development Program (BPIDP), and the Government of Ontario through the Ontario
Media Development Corporation's Book Initiative for our publishing activities.

ONTARIO ARTS COUNCIL
CONSEIL DES ARTS DE L'ONTARIO

DEDICATION
For my grandmother, whose strength and determination
is true inspiration to be a finisher in life.

ACKNOWLEDGMENTS
Many thanks to all the wonderful people at Maple Tree Press, the National Soccer
Hall of Fame, the Soccer Hall of Fame, Canada, Alexandra Kiriakos, Fraser Miller,
Paul Andrew, and Helga Haberfellner.

Cataloguing in Publication Data
Thomas, Keltie
How soccer works / Keltie Thomas ;
illustrator, Stephen MacEachern.

Includes index.
ISBN 13: 978-1-897349-00-7 (bound) / ISBN 10: 1-897349-00-9 (bound)
ISBN 13: 978-1-897349-01-4 (pbk.) / ISBN 10: 1-897349-01-7 (pbk.)
1. Soccer-Juvenile literature. I. MacEachern, Stephen II. Title.
GV943.25.T46 2007   j796.334   C2007-901791-6

Design, art direction, and illustrations: Stephen MacEachern
Photo Credits: see page 64

Printed in China

B   C   D   E   F

CONTENTS

HOW DOES SOCCER WORK?

Fans, players, and inquiring minds everywhere want to know!

What makes soccer the simplest game on Earth that requires so much skill? What makes the ball so bouncy? How do players bend the ball around a human wall? How do ground crews get the pitch absolutely perfect? Why are shoes soccer players' most important piece of equipment? How do goalkeepers cut down the angle? And what is that angle? What's the score on penalty kicks?

Well, just like everything else on Earth, it all comes down to science (plus a few things science hasn't managed to explain yet!). And if you think that makes soccer sound boring, you'd better check what planet you're on. But, hey, why don't you turn the page and check out the world of soccer in action for yourself. Whether you want answers to those burning questions, tips on becoming a better player, the scoop on inside information, or just to have a blast with the game, this book's for you.

PSSSST. YOU DON'T HAVE TO BE A SOCCER MANIAC TO READ THIS BOOK. THE RULES AND REGS AND SOCCER TALK ARE DECODED ON PAGE 61.

How Earth Became Planet Football

Has the whole world gone football crazy? You bet! Football—a.k.a. soccer in North America—has millions of players and fans all over the globe. How did people come up with such a simple game that requires so much skill? Nobody knows exactly. But different versions of it have sprung up all over the world through the ages.

In ancient Egypt, large numbers of people sometimes kicked a ball around farmers' fields to till the soil for crops. In China, ancient warriors played *tsu chu*, where players tried to score by kicking a ball through a hole in a net. In Japan, Mexico, Greece, and Rome, ancients also kicked up the dust with ball games.

In North America, First Nations played *pasuckuakohowog*, which means "they gather to play ball with the foot," and the Inuit played *Aqsaqtuk*, which means "soccer on ice." In Britain, whole villages played against each other in rough-and-tumble contests that rolled pell-mell through streets, fields, hedges, and streams. "Mob football" wreaked so much damage that British and Scottish kings banned it. But people were so crazy for football, they went right on playing anyway!

In 1863, eleven British clubs got together and wrote down the first set of rules. They said players had to handle the ball with their feet—not their hands. And those rules evolved into the modern game of soccer that the whole world knows and loves today.

Chapter 1

THAT'S THE WAY THE BALL BOUNCES

Ba-boof! Zoom!

A striker shoots on net. Fans hold their breath. Will the ball tear through the maze of players jostling in front of the goal? Will the goalkeeper reach the ball in time to make the save? Or will the ball rocket across the line for a goal?

Bonk! The ball rebounds off the goalpost into the clear. Suddenly, it's anybody's ball and both teams rush to pounce on it. But the ball is never really up for grabs. No player but the goalkeeper can play the ball with his or her hands. And that's what makes soccer—a.k.a football—unlike almost every other ball game.

Since players can't catch or throw the ball, or handle it with a bat, club, or stick, they use their body—from head to toe—to maneuver and control it. Find out what it takes for players to be so "on the ball" and what makes the ball a tricky character to put the moves on.

Head in! ➤

BALL WITH PERSONALITY

What makes this zingy character perfectly suited to the game?

IT'S ROUND

Just how do you control a round ball without using your hands at all? It's a challenge! The ball can roll, spin, or wander away from you at the slightest touch. And that's exactly why the game's rule makers chose this round shape. Trapping, kicking, heading, and moving the roly-poly sphere on the field requires players to develop awesome skills. And when players reveal these skills, making dazzling moves such as dribbling the ball through an army of defenders, they bring fans to their feet, cheering for a repeat. And so the beautiful game whirls round and round!

IT'S GOT SPOTS

The ball wears a synthetic leather jacket that's white with black spots. But this ball's no Dalmatian wannabe. Its spots help players detect swerves in its motion. The ball's jacket is made of 32 patches—20 white hexagons and 12 black pentagons. When ballmakers stitch these shapes together and pump it full of air, the shapes form an almost perfect sphere. In 1985, scientists found the same design in nature. They discovered the Buckyball—a hollow sphere of carbon atoms that remain stable, because they are arranged in the same pattern of shapes as the ball. Bucky, meet Spotty…. Now that's distinguished company!

IT'S A TV STAR

The spotted ball made its field debut in 1970 as the official World Cup ball, and became an instant TV star. No joke! Until then, the ball's jacket was white, brown, or another solid color. The addition of black spots helped fans see the ball on black-and-white TV. The Cup ball even went by the name "Telstar" for "Star of Television." Today, sports-vision scientists continue to make the ball more visible to fans and players. They have found, for example, that yellow is the most visible ball jacket color to the human eye in low light. So they developed a yellow ball with contrasting blue stripes that some teams use during the low light conditions of winter.

It Weighs In

According to FIFA (Fédération Internationale de Football Association), the ball must be "not more than 450 g (16 oz.) … and not less than 410 g (14 oz.)." If it's lighter or heavier, the ball may move differently than players expect as they kick, trap, or head it. What's more, when the ball absorbs water, it becomes heavier and behaves differently than when it's dry. It doesn't bounce as high, cuts through the air more slowly, and is more difficult for players to bend, or curve. So the ball also has to pass a water absorption test. If its weight goes up more than 10 percent when it gets wet, it's booted out before it ever gets in the game. Heavy stuff!

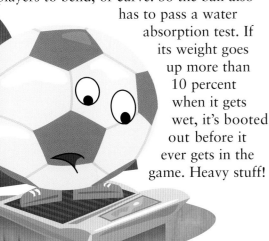

It Stays in Shape

Whomp! Whoomp! Boof! Players wallop the ball 2,000 times during the average game. It's no wonder that all pro balls have to take a shape and size retention test. Ball testers fire them against a steel plate 2,000 times at 50 km (31 miles) per hour. Only those balls that remain intact get FIFA's seal of approval. Otherwise, the ball would respond differently to the force of players' kicks at the end of the game than at the start. So players would lose ball control.

It's an Airhead

It's the air inside that gives the ball its bounce. That's because air is elastic, like a rubber band. When the ball strikes the ground, the air shrinks, so the ball squashes up slightly upon impact. Then the air expands, snapping the ball back into shape and pushing down on the ground. And since every action in our universe has an equal and opposite reaction, the ground pushes back, bouncing the ball up. The air also exerts a high amount of pressure on the ball's jacket. This pressure makes the ball feel stiff, so it's responsive to players' kicks. A well-kicked ball actually bounces off the foot and can reach a speed of 160 km (100 miles) per hour.

Tip

Play with a ball your own size. Soccer balls come in 5 sizes. Sizes 1 and 2 are the smallest balls, made for souvenirs. Size 3 is for kids under 8. Size 4 is for kids 8 to 12. Size 5, the largest ball, is made for anyone over 12, including pros!

Get Under the Ball's Skin

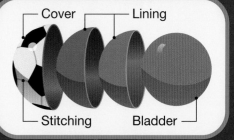

Cover | Lining | Stitching | Bladder

The ball's a perfect character for soccer inside and out. Its outer jacket is made of water-resistant synthetic leather or the like. Pro balls wear jackets that are hand-stitched or heat-bonded together rather than glued to create tighter and stronger seams. The jacket has an inner lining of four or more layers of cotton, polyester, and rubber that are bonded together. Some linings also have a foam layer that gives players extra cushioning and control. The lining strengthens the ball and helps keep its shape. Under the lining, a latex bladder holds air and gives the ball its characteristic bounce. Boing!

BOUNCING THROUGH TIME

 HECK OUT HOW THE BALL GOT ON A ROLL AND BECAME THE SMOOTH-BOUNCING CHARACTER IT IS TODAY.

2000 BC
The oldest known balls roll into the world fashioned out of wood, leather, and papyrus by the ancient Egyptians.

1697 BC
Chinese Emperor Huang-Ti invents *tsu chu*. The name of the game means "kicking a stuffed ball of animal skin," and the object is to hoof said ball through a small hole in a net hung between bamboo poles.

700 AD
Legend has it that villagers in east England play the world's first soccer game with the severed head of a Danish prince they had routed in battle! Later, animal heads and pig bladders became the ball.

1836
Charles Goodyear discovers how to harden (vulcanize) rubber with heat. The result? A rubber bladder eventually replaces the ball's pig bladder. This gives the ball a standard size and shape, easier for players to control.

CHARLES GOODYEAR
Safety Pioneer
WHO DISCOVERED VULCANIZED RUBBER 100 YEARS AGO
1839 · 1939

Around 1840
Kids at Harrow School in London, England, kick around a leather ball shaped like a giant hockey puck.

1855
Charles Goodyear makes the first vulcanized rubber soccer ball.

1863
The English Football Association is born. They hash out the first rules of the game, agreeing to call the game Association Football and that players may not use hands to handle the ball. The ball is a rubber bladder covered by panels of heavy brown leather stitched together. A row of thick laces sticks out on one side. But, strangely, the rules don't mention the ball.

1872
The English Football Association revises the rules. They say the ball must be the shape of a sphere and measure 68.6 to 71.1 cm (27 to 28 inches) all the way around—a rule that stands today!

1888
Single and married women of Inverness, Scotland, square off against each other using a pig's bladder pumped full of air, in the first recorded women's soccer match.

1888

The English Football League springs up. Soccer balls soon begin to roll off mass production lines to supply the league. But the skills of the cutters and stitchers, and the quality of the balls' cowhide covering, vary widely. So not all balls remain round.

1910

Boing! Made of an inner tube covered by thick, brown leather, the ball is lighter and bouncier but remains excellent to kick. Ballmakers insert a rubber bladder through a slit, inflate the bladder, then sew up the slit with a thick row of outer laces. But the laces make heading the ball painful and, when the leather absorbs water, the ball gets very heavy. Ouch! What's more, the leather varies in quality and sometimes tears during matches. Rip!

Around 1940

Ballmakers insert heavy-duty cloth between the ball's leather jacket and bladder. This gives the ball more strength and helps it retain its shape. The invention of a new inflation valve means no more outer laces and a coat of paint makes the ball more water resistant. Heading and dribbling become easier.

1970

Adidas rolls out the Telstar—the first official World Cup ball. The Telstar's leather jacket is made of 32 hand-stitched panels. But unlike any soccer ball before, its white jacket has black spots, or pentagons. The new design makes the ball more visible on black-and-white TV and remains the most popular ball design today.

1986

The official World Cup ball wears a synthetic leather jacket for the first time. The new jacket makes the ball more durable and cuts down water absorption. During wet game conditions, it prevents the ball from becoming heavier to kick and slower in flight. Soon synthetic leather replaces leather in soccer balls made all over the world.

2006

The official World Cup ball sports a radical new design made of 14 panels rather than 32. This cuts down the number of corners and seams between panels, turning out a rounder ball that players can handle with more accuracy and control than ever before.

Quick Kick

In the 1880s, students who liked slang coined the term "soccer." They took the name "Association Football" shortened "association" to "soc," and added "er."

Quick Answers to Speedy Questions

What's a fifty-fifty ball?

Anybody's ball! It's a loose ball both teams have an equal chance of winning if they're prepared to battle for it.

How do you nutmeg an opponent?

Dribble the ball through his legs then scoop it up with your feet on the other side of him. It's a move that's spicy, dicey, and not very "nicey"!

Beyond

Ballmakers continue their quest to make the perfect soccer ball—a ball that flies fast and accurately, absorbs no water, and transfers all the energy of players' kicks into motion.

HERE COMES THE BALL

Look out! The ball is coming straight at you. Here's how to play the ball, so it doesn't play you.

IT'S A TRAP!

The ball can rush at you a zillion different ways from a zillion different angles in a game. And you know you can't play the ball with your hands unless you're the goalkeeper. So what do you do? Depending on the ball's height, you can trap it with your feet, your thighs, your chest, or even your head. Trapping, or stopping a moving ball, is the first step to controlling it. After all, you can't shoot, pass, or score if you don't have the ball. The key to trapping is to softly cushion the ball with your body. Let your body "give" a little as it receives the ball to absorb the ball's energy. Then the ball will have less energy to rebound away from you. Once the ball strikes the inside of your foot, for example, draw your foot back to bring the ball to a stop. Gotcha!

RUN, DRIBBLE, RUN

Have ball, will travel, and elude the opposition every step of the way. That's the goal of top pros as they dribble the ball on the run. Skilled dribblers tap the ball lightly with the inside and outside of both feet. They keep the ball close enough to their feet so opponents can't steal it, but far away enough so they can zip down the field quickly. They zigzag the ball this way and that without looking down. And they're armed, or is that "footed," with slick moves—fakes, changing directions, and change of pace—that allow them to surprise, confuse, and blaze past opponents.

SICK FEATS WITH FEET

CHECK OUT SOME MOVES MADE BY DRIBBLE WIZARDS TO CONFOUND DEFENDERS:

The Elastico

When Brazil's Ronaldinho makes this move on the fly, the ball looks like it's glued to his foot. He pushes the ball one way with the outside of his foot to fake out the defender. Then he immediately brings it back with the inside of the foot—snap!— and blasts past the defender.

Carin Gabarra

The Scissors

Portugal's Christiano Ronaldo cuts holes around defenders with this move. He fakes kicking the ball with the outside of his foot then surprises opponents by stepping over the ball instead. Then he often does a "double scissors" by repeating the move with the other foot. Snip, snip!

Quick Kick

Cesar Zavala fired one of the hardest shots at the 1986 World Cup. When the Paraguayan midfielder kicked the ball over the crossbar in a match against Mexico, the ball lost all its air and had to be replaced!

Hamm on Rye, er, Ball

When it comes to dribbling, former U.S. star Mia Hamm was totally on the ball. She foiled defenders by making her body look like she was going one way. Then once the defender began to lean that way, she cut the ball back the other way and charged by the defender. Whoosh!

LEGENDS OF THE GAME

Ronaldinho's Secret Weapon

Nobody can rock and roll the ball with control quite like Ronaldinho. The star Brazilian midfielder can dribble without touching the ball and boot accurate passes without looking. Ronaldinho's feet seem to whir around the ball every which way in a dizzying blur that stops opponents from guessing his next move. And he's always inventing new moves to stymie defenders with surprise.

When he was a kid, Ronaldinho developed his first moves by experimenting with his dog Bombom. After his friends quit playing for the day, he would kick the ball around with Bombom. "I had to work hard on my moves to keep him from getting the ball," Ronaldinho told the Associated Press during the 2006 World Cup. And when it rained, the young Ronaldinho dribbled the ball past tables and chairs inside. Today, Ronaldinho still practices dribbling with his two dogs. Woof, woof!

Chapter 2

THE FIELD

Absolutely perfect!

Not a lump or bump to tip shots off course. Not a hole to trip players up. Not even a blade of grass out of place. Nothing less will do for the playing fields of the World Cup.

Soccer leagues all over the world take the quality of the pitch seriously. If a field's not up to snuff, players complain. That's because a top-notch playing surface is necessary for top-notch action. For example, the turf must be perfectly level for the ball to roll straight and true. A flat, well-groomed field with "give," or shock absorption, is also vital for players' health and safety.

And since the playing field is in the open air, teams and players may sound off about environmental conditions of the pitch, such as weather and temperature, too. Check out how the turf and its open-air environment influence the game and keep players on their toes.

Play on the grass!

THE TURF

I t's green, it's lush, and it doesn't give players any sass as they pound it into the ground with their feet. It just springs back into place ready for more action. No wonder grass is the playing surface of the pro leagues around the world. Check out how natural grass gets fit for the game.

ROLL OUT THE GREEN CARPET

R efrigerated trucks delivered the specially grown turf to all 12 stadiums in Germany hosting the 2006 World Cup. Then ground crews got to work. Laying a new pitch is a huge job that can take three days from start to finish. The crew uses a special machine to pull up the old turf, and a conveyor belt to move it into a waiting trailer. They also remove the old soil, for better drainage. Then they cover the field area with sand and use a special vehicle to mix in topsoil. Next they drive around the pitch in laps like a Formula One racecar to flatten out the top layer of soil. Otherwise, the new turf may sink about 4 cm (1 ½ in.). Then, they level out the top layer with a laser and flatten it again with a mat so the sod will settle in and take root. Finally, they roll out about 550 rolls of sod. Once that's done, they apply finishing touches and field markings.

HUSH-HUSH 'N' LUSH

P sssst. Did you know that the grass for the 2006 World Cup in Germany was grown in a top-secret location to safeguard it from pranksters and souvenir hunters? Farmers grew a blend of smooth meadow grass and rye grass chosen by FIFA and a team of experts to meet strict quality standards. The chosen blend had to thrive in the climate, let the ball roll fast, withstand trampling, and be lush green in color. After all, the playing surface influences the speed, roll, and bounce of the ball. In turn, this behavior of the ball influences the skill required to play it. Even top players can't control the ball if it doesn't roll over the field smoothly!

RIPE FOR STRIPES

A fter the new turf is laid, it's ripe for stripes. Huh? It's ready to be mowed. Believe it or not, FIFA has rules for mowing World Cup grass. The blades must be cut 2.8 cm (1 in.) high in a mowing pattern of stripes that run across the entire width or length of the field. And FIFA actually prefers stripes that flow across the width, because they help referees tell when players are offside. The ground crew create stripes by mowing the field in alternate directions. They use mowers with a roller that bends the grass in the same direction as the mower moves. Afterwards, when you look at the field, the grass bending away from you looks light green and the grass bending toward you looks dark green. That's because sunlight reflects off the entire blades of the grass bending away from you, but only off the tips of the blades bending toward you. Who knew turf was such mind-bending stuff?

TUFTS WILL FLY!

Ground crews groom the World Cup grass daily. They mow it, water it, and fertilize it, and after games, they repair it. The fact is games beat up the turf. Tufts of grass fly as players dig their cleats into the turf on the run. Sliding tackles leave their mark, and scuffles for the ball rip up the turf. So ground crews collect and remove all the torn-up bits and pieces. They fix any cleat marks, skids, and small divots by filling them with seed. They cut out big divots and replace them with new chunks of sod. And they seed any bald patches with a mix of seed and sand that's been dyed green. Once they're done, the pitch is picture-perfect and ready for action.

TRY THIS!

How much does the playing surface affect the bounce of the ball?
Try this experiment and see.

YOU WiLL NEED

• soccer ball
• metre (yard) stick
• two colors of chalk, such as green and white

1 Go outside and find a patch of grass. Have a friend put the zero-end of the yardstick on the ground and hold the stick upright.

2 Line up the bottom of the ball with the top of the yardstick. Drop the ball and notice how high it bounces next to the yardstick.

3 Mark the height of the bounce on the stick with green chalk.

4 Repeat steps 2 and 3 four times.

5 Find a patch of pavement. Repeat steps 1 to 4 but use white chalk instead of green.

6 Look at the height of the bounces you recorded on the yardstick.

Which surface would you rather play on? Grass or pavement? Why?
See answer on page 64.

TURF DOC TO THE RESCUE

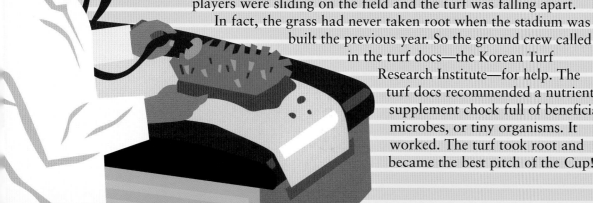

It's alive! It's true, grass is a living organism. It needs sunlight, water, and nutrients to grow and favorable soil and climate conditions to take root. And if it doesn't get what it needs, players can't count on it to "play by the rules." For example, a short while before South Korea's Daegu Stadium was about to host the 2002 World Cup, the coach of the South Korean team noticed that players were sliding on the field and the turf was falling apart. In fact, the grass had never taken root when the stadium was built the previous year. So the ground crew called in the turf docs—the Korean Turf Research Institute—for help. The turf docs recommended a nutrient supplement chock full of beneficial microbes, or tiny organisms. It worked. The turf took root and became the best pitch of the Cup!

Quick Kick

At the 2006 World Cup in Germany, groundskeepers had a handbook of instructions for looking after the turf that was 24 pages long!

SOMETHING IN THE AIR

Soccer is played in the great outdoors around the world. Check out how high altitudes—heights above sea level—different climates, and weather can influence the game.

DIZZYING HEIGHTS

Is there something about the air up there? You might ask, if you were playing in Mexico City, at 2,240 m (7,349 ft.) above the sea. Playing at high altitudes can zap your game and leave you gasping for air unless you're used to it. Air is thin at high altitudes. So you get less oxygen in each breath. When your lungs and blood get less oxygen, your heart rate goes up, and you tire more quickly. What's more, the ball zips further and faster through thin air. In 1970 and 1986, Mexico hosted the World Cup and many European teams felt that the high altitudes put them at a disadvantage. Sure, teams could arrive a few weeks early to allow their bodies to adjust, or acclimatize. And several did. But even so, they wouldn't ever be able to take up oxygen as efficiently as players born and raised at high altitudes. Them's the breaks!

Quick Kick

Nowadays, teams deal with high altitudes by taking time to acclimatize and by devising game strategies that favor their best skills. Or they arrive and play right away—before the effects of high altitude set in.

EXTREME TEMPERATURES

Extreme temperatures can burn or cast a chill over players' performances. The normal temperature of the human body is 37 °C (98.6 °F). A rise or fall of just 4 °C stymies mental and physical abilities. As the temperature drops, muscles don't react as fast as usual or with as much strength. Muscles may also cramp or spasm in the cold. So it's important for players to keep warm through warm-up exercises and extra layers of clothing. In extreme heat, players need to keep cool—and drink lots of water. In high temperatures the distance players run during matches goes down and the amount of sweat they ooze goes up—all in the body's effort to keep cool. In the 1970 World Cup at Mexico, players played in scorching 32 °C (90 °F) heat. They lost as many as 4.5 kg (10 lbs) a game in fluids. Some were even knocked out by heatstroke and sent home!

ROUGH WEATHER

Baked by sun. Pelted by rain. Blasted by wind. Blanketed by snow. Playing in the open air exposes players and the field to highly variable weather. Rain and snow make the field wet and slippery, and the ball slick to handle. This can make the game more hazardous to play and throw players off balance. In a rain-soaked game between the Ukraine and Saudi Arabia during the 2006 World Cup, a Ukraine player let a shot go from 35 m (115 ft.) out. It looked like the Saudi goalie would reach it. But then he slipped on the wet grass and the shot hurtled into the net! And sometimes shots can skid in off wet ground. Windy days can wreak havoc on the field, too. Gusts of wind can lift, swerve, and drop the ball in unexpected ways, changing the course of corner kicks and shots on goal in midair. So players—especially goalies—must be ready to roll with the weather's punches whatever they may be.

Out of This World

Is artificial turf a cut below natural turf?

The first artificial turf was a poor substitute for natural grass. It made the ball roll funny and bounce high around players' knees. And when players made sliding tackles, it gave them "rug burns" instead of cushioning the shock to their skin and bones. Nowadays, artificial turf is made especially for soccer—good for places that don't have enough sunlight, wind, and rain for natural grass to grow. The turf is tested for ball roll and bounce along with abrasiveness, slip resistance, and shock absorption. But FIFA still maintains there's no better soccer-playing surface than grass.

Talk about tough environments to play in. How about playing on a field of powdery dust that's truly out of this world? In 1972, Apollo 17 astronauts played soccer on the moon with a 91 kg (200 lb) rock! Sound heavy? The weight of objects on the moon is one-sixth of that on Earth. So the rock felt light enough to kick around like a ball.

STAR ☆

The field at the Sapporo Dome in Japan floats on air. It's the world's first natural grass movable soccer field. Instead of building a stadium roof that lets in sunlight for grass to grow, architects built an outdoor field that can glide inside on a cushion of pressurized air. That way matches can be played on natural grass without interference from rain, wind, or snow.

Sapporo Dome

TIP

Playing goal on a rainy day? Wear gloves to help you handle a wet, slippery ball.

Pitch Turns Pelé's Feet Green

"Pelé, Pelé, Pelé!" Edson Arantes do Nascimento was only 12 years old when crowds began to chant the nickname Pelé as he rushed down the field with his dancing feet. Though none of his soccer pals who gave him the nickname can say exactly what it means anymore, the name stuck.

The Brazilian forward could do it all and his mesmerizing feats captivated the world like no other. Pelé could play the ball with his right and left foot. He was awesome in the air. He could dribble the ball through an entire team of defenders for a GOOOAL. And he could leap up and play the ball with his chest to score.

In 1975, Pelé joined the New York Cosmos. After his first game on their field, his feet turned green. Yikes! Was fungus attacking his feet, Pelé wondered. Were his playing days over? It turned out the fungus was only green paint. The ground crew had covered up patches of dirt on the field with spray paint for the TV broadcast of the big game. After all, it's not every day the one and only Pelé takes the field for your team. Luckily, the paint washed off and Pelé's feet continued to dance to their goal-scoring beat.

Chapter 3

THE WEAR 'N' GEAR

Hey, let's play!

Have no fear. The game of soccer really needs no gear. All you need is a ball—and you can even play without one! In fact, you'd be in good company. Pelé, one of the greatest players ever, grew up on the streets of Brazil playing with a ball made out of a sock stuffed with rags.

You can play soccer in your everyday clothes and shoes. That's exactly what the first players did. It wasn't until the 1800s that players began wearing team uniforms and looking for equipment to protect their feet and shins during skirmishes for the ball. Today, pros wear uniforms and gear made with high-tech materials for cutting edge performance. Discover how modern uniforms keep pros cool in the heat of the action and goalkeepers gear up to guard the net.

Gear Up!

PLAYERS IN UNIFORM

Check out how modern uniforms help pros deliver their best performance on the field.

SHIRTS

Gone are the thick wool shirts pros wore in the 1900s. And the cotton shirts they wore after that, and the nylon shirts they wore in the 60s and 70s. None of them helped players stay cool during matches like the loose, polyester shirts pros wear today. Made of lightweight breathable fabric, modern shirts draw, or wick, sweat away from the skin so players stay cool and dry. Grooves in the fabric also provide space for cooling air to circulate close to players' skin. What's more, silver-coated yarns draw heat away from the body's sweat zones. Now that's cool!

SHORTS

Pros wear loose-fitting shorts so they can chase, pass, and kick the ball freely and easily. Whether soccer shorts are short or long is a matter of style. At the 2006 World Cup, some teams wore shorts slightly longer at the back than the front to help free up players' legs for sprinting. It's important for shorts to be lightweight, tear-resistant, and breathable. So today shorts are made of microfiber, not cotton, to let sweat pass through and keep players dry.

SHINGUARDS

Run your hand down your shin. Notice how you don't have much padding—a.k.a flesh—there? Early soccer players stuffed rolls of newspaper down their socks to protect their shins from opponents' hard kicks and other blows of the game. Eventually, they adapted pads from cricket to use instead. Today, all soccer players—from kids to pros—wear shinguards inside their game socks. The outer plastic shell of shinguards reduces the force of kicks and blows by spreading the energy of impact over a wide area. An inner foam layer cuts down the impact force like a shock absorber.

Quick Kick

Not much could hold Italy back from winning the 2006 World Cup. In fact, the team tested their shirts for wind drag in a wind tunnel used for testing Formula One racecars!

22

The Shirt Trade

Hey! Just take the shirt off my back, why don't you? Trading shirts after big matches is a tradition unique to soccer players that goes back to the 1954 World Cup. Some players like to collect shirts from their idols or opponents they admire. In fact, in Pelé's day, players used to fight over the legendary Brazilian striker's shirt. So Pelé always gave his shirt to the first player who asked for it. Over his career, Pelé scored goals, goals, and more goals and he began giving away shirts, shirts, and more shirts—an estimated 20,000 shirts or more. Today those number 10 shirts are collector's items as many people still say Pelé is the greatest soccer player the world has ever seen.

Socks

Do socks rock? You bet! Pro players wear knee socks with built-in support for their ankles and the arches in their feet. The socks fit snugly to increase players' feel and control of the ball. They're made of synthetic knit materials that wick away perspiration so players' feet don't get wet from sweat.

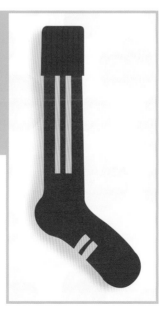

Cleats

Cleats—shoes, boots, no matter what you call them—are the most important piece of equipment in every player's kit. Cleats give players traction on the field. What's more, they're designed to help players handle the ball with the inside and outside of their feet.

Quick Answers to Speedy Questions

What's a kit?

In the United Kingdom, "kit" is the lingo for a player's entire uniform. The word for soccer shoes is "boots" over there.

How do players get capped?

Getting capped is one the game's highest honors all over the world. Players "get credited with a cap" each time they play for their country's team. Some countries give players a ceremonial cap embroidered with their team or country's colors just like the caps worn by players in the 1800s. Other countries don't. Cap that!

Why do players wear tracksuits?

Tracksuits help keep players warm and dry during cold and rainy weather. That way, players are less likely to injure or pull a chilled muscle.

TIP

Cleats will help stop you from slipping on grass. But if you're playing on artificial turf, check if cleats or regular running shoes are best for a firm footing.

A GOALIE'S GEAR

Pow! Goalies punch, kick, and catch the ball. Whomp! Goalies jump, dive, and fall, giving their all, to save the net from the ball. Oof! So goalies are kitted out with some special gear for the job.

HUMAN SHIELD

Like a human shield, goalkeepers use their whole body to stop the ball from crashing into the net. So along with the shinguards that regular players wear, goalies wear elbow pads, and some wear knee pads, too. Their uniforms also have pads built right in. Goalie shirts have built-in chest and arm pads for deflecting balls and goalie shorts have built-in hip pads for making ground-sliding stops. What's more, goalies wear special gloves to protect their hands and handle the ball. Tiny suction cups on the palms of the gloves help goalies get a grip on quick-moving shots. Some gloves even have interchangeable palm grips—one for dry ground, one for wet ground, and another for hard ground!

FASHION REBEL?

Goalkeepers have a style all their own. No joke! According to the rules of the game, goalies must stand out clearly by wearing colors that can't be confused with those of other players and game officials. In the 1990s, Mexican backstop Jorge Campos stood out like no other. Campos wore fluorescent yellow and neon-colored stripes between the posts! Another goalkeeper once wore an archery target on his uniform. What's up with the colors, stripes, and patterns? Well, some people think solid colors make goalies more difficult for shooters to see. While others think bright colors and patterns make shooters more likely to shoot at the keeper than the net. Whatever the case may be, goalies have lots of choices.

A Goalie's Turf

Goalies have a huge turf to cover. The goal stretches 2.44 m (8 ft.) high and 7.32 m (24 ft.) wide. That's twice as high and four times as wide as a hockey net! So soccer goalies have to move with the speed of a sprinter and agility of an acrobat to stay between the net and the ball. Today, the goal is made of two goalposts and a crossbar that extends between them. The goalposts and crossbar are white so they're highly visible on the field. A net attaches to the posts and crossbar to trap the ball and wipe out any doubt that a goal is scored. Long ago, the goalie's turf was narrower, but much taller. The goal had no height limit but the sky until a "tape" was stretched between the goalposts in 1865. Back then, there were no scoreboards either. Keeping track of the score was a low-tech affair. Goals were scored, or scratched, on the goalposts with a small notch. In fact, this scorekeeping method gave rise to the expression "to score a goal."

STAR ☆

It's a bird... It's a plane... It's Gigi. Italy's goalkeeper Gianluigi "Gigi" Buffon often flies through the air to make gravity-defying saves. In fact, fans nicknamed the acrobatic goalie "Superman." Sometimes, Gigi wears Superman T-shirts on game days, which makes fans cheer like crazy.

Gianluigi "Gigi" Buffon

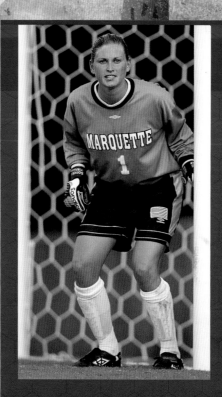

Who's #1?

Ever wondered why goalies wear the number "1"? Some people say it's because goalkeepers are the key to winning big competitions like the World Cup. After all, goalies keep the ball out of the net and many World Cup games are won or lost by a single goal. Numbers first appeared on soccer jerseys at the World Cup in 1938. Pro players were traditionally numbered by position. The goalie was number 1, the right and left backs 2 and 3, the half backs 4, 5, and 6, the right wing and right inside forwards 7 and 8, the center forward 9, and the left inside and left wing forwards 10 and 11. Once substitute players were allowed to replace starting players partway through the game, they got the number 12. Nowadays, the positions are different and players can choose their own numbers.

Look Ma, No Shorts!

"This Meazza is no center forward. This Meazza is a demon," exclaimed goalkeeper Gaviorna after being decimated 8–0 by Giuseppe Meazza and the Inter Milan squad. Not much could stop the goal-scoring "demon" from putting the ball in the back of the net. Not even losing his shorts.

During a match between Italy and Brazil at the 1938 World Cup, Meazza went to take a penalty kick and the drawstring on his shorts broke. Snap! His shorts fell to his knees. Plop! And the crowd of thousands, including Brazil's goalkeeper, burst into peals of laughter. Ha, ha!

But that didn't deter Meazza. The ace striker calmly held up his shorts with one hand and placed the ball with other. His shorts fell to the ground with his kick and the ball blew past the goalkeeper for the game-clinching goal. Meazza's teammates then rushed around to shield him from view until a new pair of shorts was found.

Chapter 4.

CLEATS FOR FEET

Have a ball,
go barefoot! Many indigenous peoples of the world who played early forms of soccer chased the ball without any shoes at all. Once footwear became available, some even preferred to play barefoot!

The first soccer boots appeared on the pitch in England during the 1800s. They were clunky clodhoppers. Back then, players laced up large, heavy boots like today's construction boots to protect their feet. What's more, some players stuck tacks or nails in the soles for traction. And players quickly found that nails could turn boots into lethal weapons. Ouch!

Early boots weighed more than twice as much as soccer cleats today. When it rained, they bogged players down. No joke! The boots soaked up water like sponges and doubled in weight. Discover how these heavy boots evolved into today's sleek cleats, designed to inject pep into a player's step.

Walk this way! ➤

CLEATS UP CLOSE AND BEAUTIFUL

C leats—shoes, boots, or whatever you call them—fit like a glove so players can feel the ball with their feet. Check out the elements that make pro cleats essential footwear for the beautiful game.

THE UPPER

The upper is made of kangaroo leather, which is soft and flexible so players can feel the ball easily. Some uppers have a cover that folds over the laces, creating a flat kicking surface to help players' shots fly straight. Some have a special coating that makes the side of the foot "stickier" to help players "bend," or swerve, the ball more when they kick it. Some also have a row of thin rubber lines on the top part of the foot to help players kick with more power and accuracy.

THE INSOLE

Many pro shoes have a foam insole to cushion players' feet and provide a tight but comfortable fit. Some also have a thin insock to absorb shocks.

THE OUTSOLE

The outsole is thin to give the shoe flexibility and hard to provide a firm surface for attaching cleats, or studs. Many shoes have built-in plastic plates between the outsole and the cleats to cut down the pressure from the individual cleats as they press into players' feet.

HEEL LOCK

The heel hugs the heel of the foot snugly to keep the foot from lifting as players step, walk, run, and kick away.

LACES

Hey laces, take your places! The laces on a standard soccer shoe go straight up the middle. But on some pro shoes, the laces curve like a banana toward the outside of the foot. This placement cuts down pressure on the top of the foot. It also prevents the laces from coming between the foot and the ball. That way the laces don't zap power from players' kicks.

MOLDED OR DETACHABLE CLEATS

Dig in to play! These bumpy knobs dig into natural turf to help players get a grip rather than wiping out. Some cleats are molded as part of the sole and others are detachable. Most detachable studs are made of lightweight metal such as aluminum or magnesium. Different studs suit different field conditions. Some studs help players grip hard ground, others soft ground that can become wet and slippery, and others soft but firm ground.

STUDS

Early studs were shaped like soup cans. Today, some studs are wedge-shaped to provide more traction on the field.

STUD PATTERNS

In the early days, soccer boots sported four studs at the front and two studs under the heel. Today, shoe designers test and arrange cleats in rows and patterns to help players accelerate quickly, feint and turn, and sidestep with power.

STUD KEY

Switch them up. Players use a stud key to remove and attach studs to their shoes.

TIP

The fanciest soccer boots on the planet won't help you play unless they're comfortable. Comfort is the most important feature of soccer shoes.

Quick Kick

Fans called Bernabé Ferreyra "The Fierce One" thanks to his powerful shot. In 1932, the Argentinean striker took off his shoes to prove to journalists that he wasn't hiding any iron bars in the toes.

The Boot Room

The Liverpool FC Boot Room, 1982.

Hard or soft. Wet or dry. Slippery, muddy, or even icy. The playing field and weather conditions of the game can vary greatly. But players need to get a firm footing no matter what. So pro teams traditionally hired "bootmen," retired players who helped players choose the right type of boot for the field and weather conditions. Bootmen looked after hundreds of pairs of boots in the Boot Room, and the Boot Room was often a meeting place, where teams worked out game strategies. Liverpool FC had the most famous Boot Room of all, a beat-up cubbyhole where trainers, coaches, bootmen, and players plotted their way to many a victory.

BOOT IT THROUGH TIME

Step up and check out how players' boots have evolved into today's form-fitting shoes.

1830 Soccer is all the rage at English public schools. Players run riot in tightly laced ankle boots that have studded soles to grip the field. The laces wrap all the way around the ankle and the ball of the foot.

1863 The rules of the game outlaw players from wearing nails, iron plates, or hard rubber spikes that stick out of the heels or soles or their boots.

1872 England and Scotland kick off the first international match. Players battle for the ball in heavy, leather ankle boots with metal studs and steel toecaps.

1909 Metal's out, leather's in! Rulemakers ban metal studs as dangerous and players begin to wear leather studs, or cleats, to grip the field.

1922 German bootmaker Adi Dassler, who gave adidas his name, experiments with studs. The end result? Detachable screw-in studs.

1937 Players wear tight-fitting shoes to feel the ball better through their shoes. The more players can feel the ball, the better they can maneuver it.

TRY THIS ▶

What's the big deal about soccer shoes? Try this experiment and see.

YOU WILL NEED

- soccer ball
- pair of comfortable sneakers
- pair of thick winter boots

1 Put on your sneakers and go outside. Try dribbling the ball from one foot to the other and watch what happens. Can you feel the ball with your feet?

2 Pick a target and shoot the ball at it 5 times. Watch what happens.

3 Put on your winter boots and repeat the first two steps.

Which footwear would you rather play with in a game? Why?

See answer on page 64.

See answer on page 64.

Quick Answers to Speedy Questions

What's the golden boot?

No, it's not a boot made of solid gold. The golden boot is an award for the "golden scoring touch" that's won by the top goal scorer of the World Cup.

1954 The German national team sets a trend when they win the World Cup wearing revolutionary new boots cut below the ankle. At the next World Cup, the majority of players show up in the cutting-edge boots.

1978 The Copa Mundial, a soft leather shoe with molded cleats, debuts at the World Cup. The shoe marches on to become the bestselling shoe of all time. In fact, many top pros wear the Copa Mundial today even though it doesn't have the latest and greatest high-tech innovations.

1994 Wanna swerve the ball? Grip and bite it like a pingpong paddle, retired player Craig Johnston tells the kids he coaches. But our boots are made of leather not rubber, the kids point out. What's more, it's raining and our boots are slippery. So Johnston superglues the rubber from a ping-pong paddle onto a pair of boots and—presto!—the design for the Predator boot, worn by David Beckham, Michael Ballack, and Zinédine Zidane, is born.

1996 The world's first soccer shoe made especially for women strolls onto the pitch.

2006 The first shoes made of interchangeable parts— an upper, sole, and studs— hit the field. By mixing and matching the parts, players can adapt the shoes to suit not only their feet but whatever weather and field conditions crop up on game day.

STAR ★ • • • • • • • •

Boot it like Beckham! David Beckham, England's midfielder known for his amazing ability to "bend" the ball into the net around a "human wall" of defenders, gets a new pair of boots every game. Each pair is custom made for his feet and sports the names of his sons, Brooklyn, Romeo, and Cruz.

David Beckham

THE NEXT STEP ❯

What will shoe designers dream up next? No one knows. But chances are their new designs will amp up players' ball control, kicking power, and acceleration.

Just how do shoe designers come up with cleats so cool they almost make players drool? It's no easy job. New shoe designs can take years to test and develop, and designers often consult top pros every few steps of the way. Get the inside scoop on their tools and trade secrets.

IS IT ROCKET SCIENCE?

Not quite. But shoe designers do use science. The spark for new designs often comes from wondering about questions such as, how can we give players more traction? How can shoes help players accelerate? Or how can shoes help players bend the ball? Then shoe designers turn to science to find materials and experiment with prototype designs to give players extra traction, acceleration, power to bend the ball, or the like.

WANTED: SPEEDY "CLEATZALES"

How can we make the world's fastest soccer shoe? That's the question Nike shoe designers put to themselves in 2003. The designers analyzed the game and found that soccer players accelerate 40 to 60 times during a game for an average of 10 m (33 ft.). What's more, the designers discovered that players accelerate in all different directions—forward, sideways, and even to change direction. So the designers set out to create a shoe that helps players accelerate.

INTO THE LAB

Research and development took two and a half years. The designers worked with some of the fastest players in the game, such as Thierry Henry and Ronaldo. The stars dropped by the lab. Then the designers analyzed how the stars ran barefoot on a treadmill and took computer scans of their feet. "I took part in the creation process from the start, in the technical aspects mostly with traction and acceleration which for me is fundamental," Ronaldo told the press.

Quick Kick

Pros have shoes custom designed to propel, protect, and cushion their feet. In fact, shoemakers have exact molds of players' feet on file.

FIELD TESTING

The designers also had the stars test prototype shoes in the field at several points during the development process. For example, Henry ran through different acceleration moves, such as cutting away from a defender to shoot, to see if he felt the shoe helped him accelerate. Henry said it did. The designers also tested how different parts of the shoe worked with Henry. For example, to measure the performance of the heel lock, they strapped an electronic box to Henry's anklebone. They wired the box to Henry's foot and the shoe to check how much Henry's heel moved as he ran. And field testing didn't stop there. The designers also had hundreds of players from all levels of soccer try out the shoe, too.

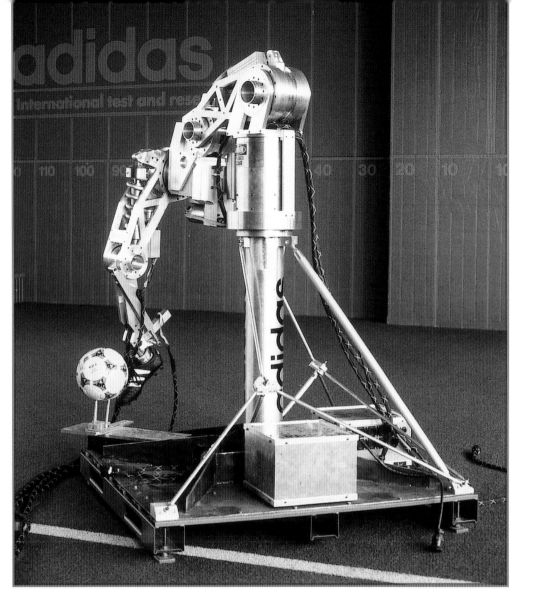

ROBOLEG KICKS IN

Sometimes, shoe designers also use a robotic leg to test out their ideas. What's up with that? Well, unlike a human, "Roboleg" can kick a soccer ball exactly the same way with the same amount of force hundreds of times. The consistency of its kicks allows designers to compare the performance of different shoes or materials. For example, when adidas wanted to make a shoe to help players bend the ball, they tested hundreds of rubber combinations on the shoe upper. So they used a robotic leg to take free kicks in order to compare the rubber combinations and find the best one.

Are Players Shoe-perstitious?

You bet some are! Check out these shoe-y superstitions and see.

Now Hear This!

Giorgio Chinaglia liked to give his shoes a pep talk before games. Maybe it fired them up. The former New York Cosmos star scored 193 goals in 213 matches, becoming the all-time scoring leader of the old North American Soccer League.

I WANT 110% FROM YOU TWO TODAY...

If the Boot Rips, Wear It

When George Hedley of the Wolverhampton Wanderers tore his boot scoring a goal in a 1908 match against Newcastle, he insisted on wearing it for the rest of the game. The striker had his favorite boots repaired 17 times before he could bear to part with them.

Reddy or Not

Wear red or go home. Maybe that was former U.S. midfielder Thomas Dooley's motto. Dooley always took to the field in red shoes.

The Miracle Boots of Bern

Wow! Check out those boots! The new boots worn by the German national team were all the talk at the 1954 World Cup. Unlike the stiff leather boots with molded studs that players traditionally laced up above their ankles, the German team's boots were made of soft leather that cut below players' ankles.

Designed by bootmaker Adi Dassler, the newfangled boots weighed half as much as regular boots. So they lightened players' load remarkably. But what really set the boots apart was Dassler's removable, screw-in studs, which could be changed to suit the field conditions.

In the final at Bern, Switzerland, Germany went toe-to-toe with Hungary—a.k.a. The Hungarian Machine, a star-packed team fans thought were invincible. Heavy rain turned the field into a muddy swamp. At half time, Dassler adjusted the Germans' boots. He replaced the shorts studs with long studs to give the players a better grip on the slippery pitch. The Germans dug in their boots to win the World Cup, 3-2. And their victory went down in soccer history as "The Miracle of Bern."

Chapter 5

THE COMPLETE ATHLETE

Zoom! They explode into a dribble, sprint down the field, and hoof rockets into the goal. They leap up to head the ball, slide along the ground to tackle opponents, and run as many as 13 km (8 miles) in a single game. Is it any wonder pro soccer players have to be in tip-top shape?

Gone are the days when players could get fit for the season by running a few laps around the track. Today, the game is much faster and players must be more physically fit than ever before. Pros train all year round to develop the speed, strength, agility, and conditioning they need to play in top form. They practice and practice to sharpen their soccer skills. And they train their minds to be just as tough as their bodies. Find out what it takes to compete as a complete soccer athlete.

Work out! ➤

Flash forward into the future: your team has made it all the way to the final game of the World Cup. The game is scoreless with only minutes left. You've been playing all out, bombing up and down the field, butting heads, and battling for the ball. Do you have enough energy left to storm your opponents' net with a flurry of shots and maybe, just maybe, score the game-winning goal?

ARE YOU FIT FOR IT?

You'd need to be in tip-top physical condition to play with the same effort and intensity at the end of the game as you did at the start. What's more, many pro games are won or lost in the last 15 minutes because physical and mental exhaustion make players prone to mistakes. Experts say that when two teams of equal skill meet, the one with better physical fitness has the edge. Not only can they play a faster game from start to finish but they can outlast their opponents. So pros need excellent physical fitness or else they may be beat without an equal chance to compete.

FITNESS = SERIOUS BUSINESS

Pros train, train, and train some more to get in shape for the game. They run wind sprints, lift weights, and play tons of soccer to develop strength, speed, agility, and endurance—the ability to go all out for an entire game. Many pro teams have strength-and-fitness coaches who develop individual player workout routines for the season and off-season. They also have speed coaches to help players improve their running skills and develop an explosive first step that may leave opponents choking on their dust.

PRACTICE MAKES PERFECT

Pros also practice game skills, running through shooting and passing drills, until they're ready to drop. But, hey, if players can practically shoot and pass in their sleep, chances are they can shoot and pass right on target when a game or even the World Cup is on the line. Pros also practice set plays, such as corner kicks and penalty kicks, over, over, and over so they can perform them flawlessly and "put the biscuit in the basket." The fact is, scoring on set plays wins many a game.

Quick Kick

Players often lose as many as 4 L (7 pints) of fluid during a game, which can lead to dehydration. Then players tire easily and are prone to mental mistakes. So pros drink lots of fluids.

The Fuel

How do pros fuel up to play at the top of their game for 90 minutes or more without running on empty? They eat a high-energy diet in the following "pro-portions":

60 to 75% carbohydrates—Cereals, breads, pasta, fruits, and veggies are players' main source of energy. Carbohydrates fuel up players for intense exercise. They help players keep going all out without running out of energy during the last 30 minutes of the game, when many goals are scored.

15 to 20% proteins—Proteins from lean beef, chicken, fish, eggs, grains, nuts, and seeds help players build and repair their muscles.

15 to 20% fats—Fats from red meat, cheese, eggs, milk, butter, salad dressing, nuts, and seeds get stored in the body as potential energy. Once carbohydrate energy gets low, fats begin to supply energy. They also help muscles develop and provide a protective cushion for players' inner organs.

Pro teams often eat a meal together three or four hours before a game. That way, they can fuel up their energy tanks without risking mechanical, or digestive, trouble. Team meals may include chicken or fish, pasta, and vegetables. According to one study, potatoes boiled for 20 minutes are a perfect pre-game food. Not only do potatoes contain carbohydrates—simple sugars that provide a steady flow of energy to players' muscles— they also contain valuable vitamins.

Check out how brainy computers are helping players prevent injuries before they happen so players don't miss lots of game time action.

POP GOES THE KNEE-O

Fernando Redondo (right) was at the very top of the game in 2000. The star Argentinean midfielder led Spanish club Real Madrid to victory and was named the league's Most Valuable Player. He transferred to Italian club AC Milan for a three-year $50 million contract and fans of Real Madrid rioted in the streets. And that's when Redondo's unfortunate tale of mystery and injury began. Three days after signing the contract, the superstar's knee gave out as he was training on a treadmill. AC Milan couldn't believe it. The team's medical staff had examined Redondo from head to toe before signing the contract and said he was in perfect condition. Over the next two years, Redondo had three knee operations to no avail. And because he couldn't play, he refused his pay.

Quick Kick

Did legendary superstar Pelé see the game better than opponents? Maybe so. In 1966, tests showed that Pelé's peripheral vision was 30 percent better than that of the average athlete.

TIP

What's the best way to prevent injuries in soccer? Warm up and stretch your leg muscles before you play or practice. Stretching your muscles regularly will develop flexibility. And research shows that the more flexible players are, the less prone they are to injuries!

MONEY ALMOST WALKS

But if Redondo had taken his wages, AC Milan would have been out millions of dollars with none of the superstar's dazzling play to show for it. The club was determined not to take such a financial risk again. So they set up a project to predict players' injuries better. And the Milan Lab was born—the world's first scientific research centre at a soccer club. The lab uses advanced computer systems and software to monitor each player's physical and mental condition and collect information during their workouts. Every two weeks a team of doctors and scientists tests individual players for speed, strength, resistance, diet, and presence of iron and vitamins. They feed all the results into a neural net— a computer system that works like a human brain. And the "brainy" computer translates the data into predictions of how likely the players are to get injuries.

COMPUTER TALKS

The brainy computer tells the staff whether the player should "stop, watch, or go." A picture of the player's body appears on a computer screen and lights up like a traffic light. If the body turns red, the computer says "the player is at risk of injury" and staff stop the player from training and playing. If the body turns yellow, the computer says "be careful" and staff watch the player carefully as he trains and plays. If the body turns blue, the computer says the player is "good to go." Thanks to the brainy system, in two years, AC Milan cut its muscular injury rate by a whopping 90 percent. Soccer clubs around the world have begun visiting the Milan Lab to learn their secrets of preventing injuries. One day, team doctors may be able to use computers like this to prevent out-of-the-blue, career-ending injuries like Fernando Redondo's before they happen.

THE MIND

Imagine this: all eyes are on you. You are about to take a penalty kick. The only player between you and the goal is the goalkeeper. Without another goal your team will be eliminated from the World Cup. They've picked you to come through in the clutch—and shoot a rocket by the goalie. Think you can do it?

THE LITTLE PLAYER THAT COULD

Several research studies show that athletes' thoughts and self-talk—things they say to themselves as they play—influence their success. In fact, some experts say the most important quality of a soccer player is not speed, strength, or a powerful shot but mental toughness— confidence and the ability to handle the ups and downs of your game. Say you botch an easy chance to score, for example. Or you give away a pass to an opponent who then scores. If you have mental toughness, you can shrug off your mistake, stay focused, and keep playing your best. But if you don't have mental toughness, you may get down on yourself and let the mistake wreck your performance for the rest of the game.

SEE IT TO BELIEVE IT

So pro players train their minds just like they train their bodies. Players work with sports psychologists to turn negative thoughts into positive ones. That way, players develop habits of thinking that allow them to play with confidence and use that speed, strength, or powerful shot of theirs to advantage. Sports psychologists also help players rehearse plays mentally through visualization. When players visualize a play, they see mental pictures of themselves making the play successfully over and over. The idea is that these mental pictures take root in their mind, so they can make the play instinctively during games. And studies show that athletes who do visualization along with physical practice outperform those who do physical practice only. Mind blowing, or what?

Quick Kick

Before the 1999 Women's World Cup, the sports psychologist of the U.S. women's national team made videotapes of highlights of each player. The team watched a few each night before the tournament. Though no one knows what effect watching the tapes had, the U.S. won the Cup.

STAR ☆

Does Ronaldinho mind passing the ball? You bet! But not the way you may think. The awesome playmaker imagines mental pictures of the best way to pass to teammates. He even considers whether a teammate likes to receive the ball at or ahead of his feet.

Ronaldinho

GOTTA HAVE HEART ♥

♥

Sure, you need to be physically fit and mentally tough to succeed at soccer. But you also have to have a strong desire to play. The fact is, if you really want to play, you'll do whatever it takes to get yourself in tip-top shape and develop the necessary skills to compete on the field.

Take Michelle Akers (right), legendary superstar of the U.S. women's national team. Akers had the desire not only to play but also to become a goal scorer—a.k.a. finisher. She spent hours shooting at the net, shooting at garbage cans in the net, shooting at cones in the net, and then a goalie. And she didn't stop there. She then added a couple of defenders into her shooting drill and began training herself to look toward the goal every time she got the ball. Her desire and hard work paid off. Akers became a top finisher in the game.

What's more, Akers' desire to play helped her battle back into first-rate shape after numerous injuries and even exhausting bouts with the illness of Chronic Fatigue Syndrome. In fact, in 2000, FIFA recognized her outstanding play by naming Akers "Women's Player of the Century."

Quick
Answers to
Speedy
Questions

What's the "warrior mentality"?

The U.S. women's national team is famous for mental toughness that ignites fear in the hearts of opponents. The team plays with an unshakable belief in themselves that they call the "warrior mentality." U.S. goal-scoring great Mia Hamm once described it as "Nothing bothers us. Nothing gets in our way of being the best."

The Mind Room

Some of Italy's best players who won the battle for the 2006 World Cup may have had a secret weapon in the mind game. They trained in the Mind Room. Italy's pro team AC Milan set up the Mind Room to gain a mental edge on opponents by training players to focus on getting "into the zone" of peak performance. Players lie on reclining chairs where they hook up to a device that measures their brain waves, muscle tension, breathing, and heart rate. Then they learn how to relax mentally and stay relaxed as they watch videos of their own mistakes—something that usually makes them tense up. Sports scientists think this training helps players reach this state of mind to deliver their best performance when they face nerve-wracking challenges in games.

TIP

Set a goal to help you grow as a player. Pick a goal that requires effort for you to achieve but is one you can reach, such as learning to dribble with both feet or making it onto the league team.

The World's Best Player

Mia Hamm had it all. The goal-scoring sparkplug of the U.S. women's national team from 1987 to 2004 could cut holes in opponents' defenses, dribble circles around defenders, feather perfect passes to teammates, and pound the ball into the net from anywhere on the field. Hamm had a champion's dedication to training and physical fitness and an insatiable desire to win.

Is it any wonder coaches, players, and fans alike declared her the world's best player? Hamm won the World Cup twice and a pair of Olympic gold medals. Along the way, she racked up a record-setting 158 international goals, becoming the all-time leading scorer of women's and men's soccer.

One time, when the U.S. goalie got injured and the team had used all its subs, the fearsome finisher even stepped between the posts to defend the goal. And in typical Hamm style she came through in the clutch.

But what Hamm had more than anything was a joyous love of the game. "It was always my love of the game, not the trophies or accolades, that kept me going for the goal," Hamm says in her book *Go for the Goal*.

Chapter 6

THE SCIENCE OF EXPLOSIVE MOVES

Wa-whoosh!

A player lets a shot rip from 36.5 m (40 yards) out, and the shot finds the back of the net. "GOOOOOAL!" The crowd erupts, hopping to their feet as the player does a little dance and her teammates mob her for joy. Is anything more exciting than the on-field action of soccer? Not likely.

Froomp! A long pass rockets toward a striker faster than any player can run the ball up field. Without missing a beat, the striker connects and drives the ball past the keeper. Vroom! Turn-oom! Boom! A free kick bends around a human wall of defenders. Then it changes direction in midair, curls back toward the net, and beats the keeper. Boing! A player jumps up, up, and away and hits the ball with his head—bop!—for a goal. Whoa! Check out the science behind soccer's explosive moves.

Heads up! ➤

THE KICKER WAS...

The players' feet. No kidding! Check out how players use their feet to feed perfect passes to teammates, blast shots past the keeper, and keep opponents guessing.

THE INSTEP KICK

To make long passes, fire hard shots, and clear the ball as far away as they can from their net, players kick with their instep—top of the foot between their ankle and toes. They plant their nonkicking foot beside the ball, pointing at the target. They draw their kicking foot back, bringing the knee over the ball. Then, with their toes pointing down and their ankle locked, they swing their kicking foot forward to strike the ball with the top of their foot. The swinging action and large striking area of the foot give the kick its power.

THE OUTSIDE FOOT KICK

Players use the outside of the foot to get passes or shots away quickly. It's a useful trick, er, kick when they don't have the time to swing through an instep kick.

THE PUSH PASS OR SHOT

When players need accuracy—not power—they kick the ball with the inside of the foot. Since this area of the foot is flat, it allows players to deliver short passes and shots right on target.

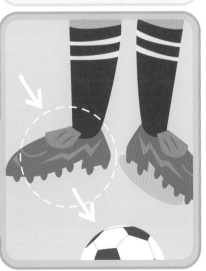

THE BACK HEEL

How do players use their back heel to be a real heel? They step over the ball and pass it to a teammate behind them by striking it firmly with the back of their heel. It's a great move to surprise opponents who are closely guarding them—especially when no teammates up front are open for a pass.

When Kara Lang lets a shot fly, look out. The crack Canadian midfielder can score from anywhere on field. Lang's powerful blasts have blown by goaltenders from as far as 24 m (80 ft.) out. "I've never seen a man hit a ball that hard," coach Even Pellerud once said.

Kara Lang

How Players Flip for Bicycle Kicks

Ever seen a player do a backflip, volleying the ball over her head, as she appears to ride an invisible bicycle in midair? The bicycle kick is the flashiest move in the game—and the diciest. It's not recommended for beginners or hard fields. It requires perfect timing. And it takes practice, a coach, and a mattress-cum-crash pad to learn. Pros jump up, throwing their non-kicking foot into the air, and fall back, striking the ball over their head with their kicking foot. Then they land softly, cushioning themselves with their hands. You might say they take the ball and the fans for a ride...

USE YOUR HEAD

Up, up, and a-wham! A player jumps up into the air and heads the ball. In soccer, the ball can spend as much time in the air as it does on the ground. So here's how to use your head like a pro.

1. Be the Striker
Keep your mouth shut and your eyes on the ball. Strike the ball—don't let the ball strike you. Hold your arms out for balance and pull your upper body back.

2. Strike While the Ball Is Loft
Leap up and push your upper body forward toward the ball. At the top of your jump, strike the ball with the center of your forehead just below your hairline. This flat bony surface that protects your brain is one of the hardest parts of your body. Use it to propel the ball to whatever target you choose.

3. Up and Over
Want to send the ball *up* into the air over a long distance? Head it on its lower half to thrust it up and out.

4. Down and In
Want to send the ball *down* so it bounces into the goal? Head it on its upper half.

Y ou're racing down the field toward the net with the ball. A defender sticks his foot out in front of you. Trip! You fly face first into the turf. Luckily, the ref sees the foul and gives your team a free kick. Now you're taking the kick for your team! Your opponents have built a human wall, standing shoulder to shoulder to block your shot on the net. What are your options? You can pass the ball to a teammate to shoot. You can shoot the ball over the wall, aiming at a spot on net. Or you can try to bend it like Beckham—shoot the ball around the wall into the net. Check out the moves and science behind *bending* the ball.

1 KICK IT OFF

S ay you want to bend, or curl, the ball to the left. Kick the ball slightly off center— toward its righthand side—with the inside of your right foot. (If you want to bend the ball to the right, do the opposite. Kick the lefthand side of the ball with the inside of your left foot.)

2 SEE BALL SPIN

B y kicking the ball off center like that, you give the ball spin. It spins counter- clockwise—in the opposite direction of the hands on a clock.

3 GO WITH THE FLOW

A s the spinning ball zips toward the net, air flows over it. See how the air moves in the opposite direction of the righthand side of the ball? This raises the air pressure there on the ball. Likewise, see how the air moves in the same direction as the lefthand side? This lowers the air pressure there.

4 WRAP YOUR HEAD AROUND IT

S ince the air pressure is lower on the lefthand side of the ball than the righthand side, the ball moves, or "bends," to the left in midair. How that's for a mind-bending shot?

It's a banana... It's a boomerang... It's a GOOOAL!

Sure, bending the ball is cool. Then there's the banana kick that Brazilian defender Roberto Carlos (right) let go in a game against France in 1997. Carlos took a free kick from about 30 m (98 ft.) out. The ball was slightly to the right of center of France's net. The French built a human wall five players wide about 10 m (33 ft.) in front of the ball. Carlos took a running start and blasted the ball with the outside of his left foot. The ball veered way off to the right, clearing the wall by a metre or more. A ball boy to the right of the net even ducked his head! Many people thought Carlos had bungled the shot. But then it swerved all the way back to the left and into the net. No one was more surprised than the French goaltender. The Brazilian team went bananas. The world was dumbfounded. How could the ball swerve so far right then almost magically go back to the left? Carlos said he practiced this kick regularly in training. And scientists think he kicked the ball so hard with the outside of his foot and gave it so much spin that he increased the bending force. Just call it a "boomergoal"!

goalie

defenders

Quick Answers to Speedy Questions

How fast do shots fly?

Experts say the fastest shots are usually clear shots on goal, such as penalty kicks. During the 1996 European Championships, the average speed of penalty kicks in a penalty shootout between England and Germany was 113 km (70 miles) per hour. Möller had the fastest shot, which sped toward the net at 129 km (80 miles) per hour.

TIP

Want to bend the ball with an instep kick? Instead of kicking the ball straight on with your laces, kick the ball slightly off center with the right or left side of your laces.

47

Flag of Uruguay

Striker Takes a Corner and Scores

Even today people don't believe it when they see it. A player takes a corner kick and scores without any other player touching the ball. It's rare, it takes lot of skill, and, in 1924, when it had never been done before, it caused an uproar.

The Uruguay national team had just returned home as the Olympic soccer champions of the world, when their old rival Argentina challenged them to a friendly match. The game was scoreless until Argentina's Cesáreo Onzari did the unthinkable. Onzari took a corner kick and booted the ball directly into the net—WHAM!

The singular goal stunned the Uruguayans. At first, they didn't say a word. Then they protested vociferously. They said their goalkeeper had been shoved when the ball was in the air. They claimed that Onzari hadn't aimed for the net at all and that the wind knocked in the ball. But the referee didn't buy any of it and let the goal stand. Rightly so. And maybe Argentina had the last word. They won the "friendly" 1-0 with what they called the "Olympic goal," and the name still stands for the remarkable goals today.

Chapter 7

STRIKER VS. GOALIE

GOOOAL! Everybody knows the object of soccer is to score goals. But soccer is a low scoring game. Getting the ball past 10 opponents and a goalkeeper isn't easy.

So when a striker takes a penalty kick 11 m (12 yards) in front of the opposition's goal without any players allowed to come between him and the goalie, everybody holds their breath. A penalty kick is a scoring chance like no other. It gives the striker a clear shot on goal and pits the striker and goalie face to face in a duel of wit, skill, and nerves.

Likewise, everybody holds their breath when a striker zips away on a breakaway on goal. Will she beat the goalie to score? Or will the goalie make the save? When a striker and a goalie face each other one-on-one, it's a battleground where games can be lost or won. Check out the science behind some of their winning moves.

Showdown Dead Ahead!

THE PENALTY KICK

It's over in less than half a second. Yet it often decides which side wins the game. Is it any wonder penalty kicks require nerves of steel for pro strikers and goalkeepers alike?

WHO? ME?

Ever noticed that "Who?-Me?-look" players get when the ref calls them for tripping or fouling in the penalty area in front of their net? Maybe that look comes from the desire not to put their team in the hole by giving their opponents an easy goal. After all, the ref then gives their opponents a penalty kick, or clear shot on goal. During a penalty kick, all players except the striker and goalie must keep out of the penalty area until the striker kicks the ball. What's more, the goalie must remain on the goal line until the ball is kicked. So she cannot move forward to cut down the angle (see far right). She may only move from side to side along the goal line. And these rules seem to favor the striker as experts say that 75 percent of penalty kicks score.

WHO YA PICKING ON?

Teams can pick any player to take a penalty kick. And their best scorer is not always the best pick. In fact, some top scorers get butterflies in their stomach if they're chosen. They don't want to crack under the pressure of having to score one for the team. So teams often pick their "penalty-kick specialists," players who have nerves of steel and a reliable, accurate shot regardless of the number of goals they've scored.

STRIKER

SHOOT TO SCORE

When a penalty-kick specialist steps up to take a penalty kick for the team, he doesn't worry about the goaltender. He knows he has the advantage, because he knows exactly where he's going to shoot the ball and the keeper doesn't. Pros often aim at a corner of the net. That way the goalie has to leap up or dive down to the ground to make the save. Then the striker winds up and drills it. Bombs away!

A SCIENTIST TAKES THE KICK

The findings of scientist Ken Bray show shooting at a corner is a good strategy. Bray studied footage of big games over the last 50 years and used biomechanics—the science of how the human body moves—to calculate the absolute reach of a goaltender diving for the ball. And he found an area near the net's top corners and posts that goaltenders can't reach—the "unsaveable zone."

Quick Kick

One study shows that where strikers point their standing foot is a clue to where their penalty kicks will go. In 85 percent of cases, the standing foot points in the direction of the shot.

GOALKEEPER

MAKE THE SAVE

How does a pro goalie play a penalty kick with the odds so stacked against him? He may try to psych out the striker by taking time to get into position on the goal line, staring the shooter down, or wishing the shooter luck. Then the keeper watches the striker carefully for clues about the shot. Is the striker looking at one side of the net? Does the striker favor shooting with his left or his right foot? Has he faced this shooter before? Does the shooter favor a particular shot on penalty kicks? Clues like these can give the goalie a chance to make the save.

A SCIENTIST BETWEEN THE POSTS

Even so, the goalie may have to guess at the shot and dive left, say, before the shot's taken only to have the shooter shoot right. Oops! Though guessing incorrectly may look stupid, moving before the shot is a smart strategy. Scientist Ken Bray found that if a goalie waits to move until after the shot, the shot will be halfway to the net before he can react. What's more, when a goalie guesses correctly and makes the save, he looks like a soccer brainiac.

TIP

Playing goal? Be alert and adjust your position so your body is always between the ball and the net. Try to see where the ball is going and move there quickly to block the shot.

Cutting Down the Angle

Sure, goalies have to stay on the goal line until a shooter shoots a penalty kick. But that doesn't mean you have to hang out there all the time during games. When a sharp shooter gives your defense the slip and closes in on net, you can cut down the angle by moving forward toward the ball. Check out the science of cutting down the angle:

The closer to the goal line you stay, the more net you leave open for the shooter to shoot at.

When you move forward from the goal line toward the ball, you take away some room to shoot at. So the shooter has less net to shoot at and may be forced to shoot wide or high.

One-on-one breakaways are exciting and nerve-wracking. Suddenly, it's just you against the keeper—or you against the striker. Playing a breakaway is like facing off in a duel of clashing wills and skills. So don't lose your nerve. Be prepared:

THE STRIKER

WHERE'S THE GOALIE?

Is he hovering on the goal line ready to spring any which way? Is he moving out toward you or falling down to the ground? Is he guarding one post so the area beside the other post is wide open to score? Knowing the goalkeeper's position can help you find openings to shoot at and decide what type of shot to take. Can you dribble around the goalie or chip the ball over his head into the net? Or can you bury the ball in a corner? When you see an opening, stuff it with your shot!

SHOOT LOW

Sure, there are times to shoot high— aiming for a top corner or a hole that opens up above the goalie. But many a time shooting low is the way to go. Low shots won't fly over the crossbar. What's more, low shots are tough for keepers to handle because their hands are usually up in the air somewhere above their knees. And keepers may not get down to the ground in time to save a low shot.

Quick Kick

Deadly striker Eric Wynalda of the U.S. men's national team once said that he scored 80 percent of his goals with low shots.

FOLLOW YOUR SHOT FOR REBOUNDS

Remember this: you are a finisher—a.k.a. goal scorer. That means you aren't finished until the ball is held fast between the goalie's hands, out of bounds, or in the back of the net. Every shot may bounce back, or rebound, off the goalie, the crossbar, or a post. So *always* follow your shot. That way you can scoop up any rebound and another chance to score.

HANG TOUGH

Being a finisher isn't easy. In fact, some coaches say only 1 out of every 10 shots fired will score. So don't get down on yourself. Chances are your shots will miss over and over. Shake off missed shots with a roll of your shoulders and believe that you'll plant the ball in the net the very next chance you get.

THE KEEPER

CUT DOWN THE ANGLE

It may not look as spectacular as flying across the net in a saving dive. But cutting down the angle (see page 51) is one of the best moves you can make when a striker zooms in on your net. As you move toward the ball from the goal line, you close up the holes where the striker can take aim. But keep your wits about you, for your timing and positioning are key. Move out too early and the shooter may be able to dribble around you for a goal. Move out too far and he may be able to chip the ball over your head to score.

STONEWALL YOUR OPPONENT

As your opponent breaks in, keep your body between the ball and the net just like you do throughout the action of the game. Stay on your feet as long as you can to pressure her to shoot. Then you can leap up, drop down, or shuffle either way to block the shot. If she shoots low, dive sideways to form a long wall with your body and your legs and then smother the ball. Drop to the ground with your hands first by leading with your palms and looking through the space between your arms. That way you can use your hands and arms to protect your face.

DON'T GIVE UP REBOUNDS

Try to smother or catch the ball and hold on tight. Pull the ball into your body so you don't give the striker a rebound—another chance to score. If you can hold onto the ball whenever you make a save, you'll stop rebound shots before they have a chance to happen.

BOUNCE BACK

Make the save and you'll feel great. But don't get down on yourself if you don't. Remember this: every goalkeeper gets scored on. You need to be mentally tough and bounce back into action. The very next save you make may clinch the game for your team. Try shaking off the goal with a roll of your shoulders or flick of your wrist. Then concentrate on keeping your body between the ball and the net—ready to pounce.

STAR ☆

Wayne Rooney plays with no fear. The sharp-shooting striker muscles and hustles his way to find the perfect place at the right time to score goals. And he's not afraid to score any way he can. Rooney scores on his own upfront, by firing blistering shots from a distance, getting on the end of crosses, and by nailing free kicks to the back of goal.

Wayne Rooney

Pelé Robbed by Banks

England and Brazil were going head-to-head in a match at the 1970 World Cup. Brazil was on the attack. But England's goalkeeper, Gordon Banks, wasn't giving up any goals. He was playing true to his nickname "Banks of England" for "being as safe between the sticks as money in the bank."

Brazil's captain Carlos Alberto fired a low pass down the right field for Jairzinho. The quick Brazilian winger picked up the pass and whipped past English defender Terry Cooper. Banks tracked Jairzinho all the way, covering the near post of the net. Then Jairzinho crossed the ball toward the far post, where Pelé was thundering in.

The cross swooped high in the air and dipped. Pelé headed it perfectly, smashing the ball low and hard toward the far post. The crowd gasped. Everyone thought the goalkeeper didn't have a chance, including Pelé who chortled "GOOOOAL." But maybe Banks didn't agree. The agile goalie dove across the net.

And somehow he managed to get his right hand on the ball. Banks flicked the ball and it floated up, up, and over the crossbar. Pelé was stunned. He said it was the greatest save he had ever seen and, to this day, the rest of the soccer world agrees.

Chapter 8

THE WORLD'S GAME

"Olé! Olé!" chant millions of World Cup fans. Not much inspires as much passion and excitement in people as the World Cup competition. Maybe that's because soccer is the only major sport played in some countries. In others, it's the only sport that seems to matter.

Countries put national pride on the line at the World Cup, sending their very best players to compete against the top players on Earth. For players, playing for their country is the highest honor. And they go all out. The fact is, once the opening round is over, teams must win each game or go home. And the chance to win the Cup comes only once every four years.

Fans go all out, too. They wear their national team's colors, and even paint their faces the team colors. Discover how playing styles of different countries have shaped the modern game and how strange events can lead to heart-stopping action at the World Cup.

Watch the beautiful game

COUNTRIES OF INVENTION

Sure, soccer is a global game today, with players of many nationalities often playing together on the same team. But when countries meet to compete at the World Cup, they often still play with some of the distinctive styles they invented years ago. Check out some of the tactics of great soccer nations that continue to shape the modern game.

ENGLAND'S SECRET WEAPON

When the English Football Association wrote the game's first rules in 1863, teams' only tactic was to score. Nine forwards would trail behind a teammate who tried to dribble the ball through defenders' lines. It wasn't much of a team effort. The forward pass to a teammate didn't exist until 1866 when the Scots took advantage of a rule change to invent it. And it turned soccer into a team game. Around 1883, northern England's Blackburn Olympic team invented a new variation—the long pass. It was their secret weapon, and they unleashed it to beat southern England's reigning champs of the F.A. Cup. The long pass caught on with teams all over England. It gave players a quick way to move the ball long distances over fields that were often muddy and soaked with rain, and bypass defending midfielders along the way. And even though long airborne passes aren't a secret anymore, England's national team still uses them as a lethal weapon.

DUTCH PLAY TOTAL SOCCER

You can play defense or you can play offense—or you can play "total soccer," where every player can cover any position. The Dutch national team whirled around opponents this way at the 1974 World Cup. Practically the whole team rushed up the field to attack. And when they lost the ball, the whole team dropped back to defend. The Dutch played total soccer all the way to the final, where they lost to the Germans, 2-1. Experts say the Dutch national team was the best team that didn't win the Cup. And though teams around the world didn't necessarily adopt total soccer, they saw how valuable such versatile players were and began to favor them. Today, defenders must have the same shooting and ball handling skills as attackers and attackers must have the same player-to-player marking, or covering, skills—to make a switch from offense to defense lickety-split.

ITALY'S LOCK

Don't want to lose games? Just lock out your opponents' offense. That was the defense strategy invented by Italy. Around 1900, teams all over the world played an attacking game. Players took a pyramid formation with 2 defenders in front of the goalie, 3 midfielders, and 5 forwards to storm their opponents' goal. The pyramid was the standard formation for about 50 years. Around 1950, Italy turned the pyramid on its head to create the *catenaccio or lock*. *Catenaccio* means "great big chain"—chain of defenders, that is. Italy used 4 defenders in front of the goalkeeper and a *libero,* or free man, behind them to close up any breaks in the chain, 3 midfielders, and only 2 forwards. The *catenaccio* locked up opponents' offense so well that it led to low-scoring games, and inspired teams around the world to focus on defense. And Italy still plays defensively today. They wait for opponents to make a mistake. Then they jump on the opportunity, sending forwards in to try to score.

BRAZIL'S ATTACK ARTISTS

"Low scoring! Downright boring!" Chances are you won't hear such complaints about Brazil. Unlike Italy and other countries that favor defense, Brazil has always gone on the attack. Once they get their feet on the ball, the Brazilians are like artists in motion. They dribble, head, trap, and pass the ball so well that their spontaneous moves flow from one to the next like well-rehearsed dance moves. The Brazilians are also players of invention. They perfected the bicycle kick and invented a kick to bend a ball around a defensive wall. In 1958, they won the World Cup with a 4-2-4 formation—4 defenders, 2 midfielders, 4 forwards—that was the talk of the world. Two of the defenders routinely zipped up field to join the attack, and experts said the formation was weak on defense. But Brazil spent so much time on offense, it didn't matter. What's more, Brazil's attack artists, then and now, were so good that the team probably could have won no matter what formation they played.

TIP

Try to score first. In the World Cup, the team that scores the first goal of the game goes on to win 77 percent of the time.

Quick Answers to Speedy Questions

What's futbol?

Soccer—what else?! Soccer is called *futbol* in Spanish, *football* in England, *le football* or *le foot* in French, and *calcio* in Italian.

What's a formation?

It's the way a team lines up its players at the beginning of the match. The 4-4-2 formation—4 defenders, 4 midfielders and 2 forwards—is popular today along with the 5-3-2 formation. (Because goalies stay in the same position, they're not counted in formations.) But once the action gets underway, the fluid nature of the game and quick shifts from offense to defense require players to range freely over the field, without sticking fast to their positions.

ELEPHANTS GET THEIR KICKS

The World Cup isn't the only heavy competition around. In 2006, 11 soccer players in Thailand kicked off against 11 elephants. The players battled the pachyderms, which were guided by human riders, to a 3-3 draw. Not bad considering Asian elephants can stand up to 3 m (10 ft.) tall and weigh in as much or even more than a mini van. In Thailand, elephants also play soccer against each other. The giant beasts of soccer hoof around a giant-size ball!

GOAL OR NO GOAL?

Check out some of the strange goings-on that have sparked controversy at the World Cup and the solutions science offers for fair play.

A TALE OF TWO BALLS

My ball or let's brawl! When archrivals Uruguay and Argentina met in the first World Cup final in 1930, both brought their own ball and insisted it be the one to play. Not wanting to choose sides, the referee hit upon a solution: Argentina's ball for the first half and Uruguay's for the second. Sound fair? Well, playing with their ball, Argentina grabbed the lead, 2–1 in the first half. Then once Uruguay got their feet on their own ball in the second half, they roared back with 3 unanswered goals to win the Cup, 4–2.

ONE BALL FOR ALL

Nowadays, the World Cup has one official ball made especially for the competition. All teams receive a shipment of official balls beforehand. That way they all have the same amount of time to train with the ball and get used to it. Sound fair? Well, the official ball of the 2006 World Cup sported a radical new design— 14 panels shaped like propellers rather than the usual 32 hexagon- and pentagon-shaped panels. And it got both players and scientists hopping. Goaltenders said it was tougher to handle. And scientists agreed. They said that shooters could bend, or swerve, the new ball more than usual and that it sometimes flew unpredictably like a knuckleball in baseball. All of which made many people think more goals would be scored. But as it turned out, the 2006 World Cup was one of the lowest scoring Cups of all time. Go figure!

Whoa! Did the ball cross the line? That's what everyone wondered at the 1966 World Cup final, when English striker Geoff Hurst ripped a blast past German goalie Hans Tilkowski in extra time. The shot struck the bottom of the crossbar, dropped straight down to the ground, and bounced out of the net. Even the referee wasn't sure whether the ball had crossed the line. He consulted the line officials and then delivered his verdict: GOAL! The English fans went wild, the Germans went ballistic, and Hurst went on to score again. England won the cup, 4-2, and the game-winning goal proved to be the most controversial goal in soccer history. Later, replays could not prove that the whole ball had crossed the line for a goal. But, as everyone knows, what the ref says goes.

Quick Kick

In 1966, thieves stole the original, solid gold World Cup trophy. Scotland Yard hunted for it high and low. But the trophy didn't turn up until a week later, when Pickles the dog sniffed something funny in a garden and dug it up.

SMART BALL TALKS TO REF

Sure, anything can happen in soccer and controversial decisions are part of the game. But one day a "smart ball," or another kind of goal line technology, may help referees tell whether the whole ball has crossed the line to score. The company that makes the official ball of the World Cup has developed a smart ball system that "talks" to the ref. The system uses sensors next to the pitch to track the movement of the ball over the goal line.

When the whole ball crosses the line, an electronic chip inside the ball sends a signal—bzzzzt—to an earpiece worn by the ref. Then the ref can signal a goal even if he couldn't see exactly what happened. How's that for telling the ref like it is?

Holy head-butt, Zidane! In the 2006 World Cup final, Zinédine Zidane made one of the most controversial moves of his career. He rammed his head into the chest of Italian defender Marco Materazzi in response to an insult and was red-carded out of the game. Nevertheless, the French midfielder won the Golden Ball award as the Cup's best player for his outstanding play that drove France all the way to the final.

Zinédine Zidane

Goalie Socks It to Strikers

Uh, oh! It's time for a penalty kick shootout. During the quarterfinal match between Germany and Argentina at the 2006 World Cup, the score remained tied after 30 minutes of extra time. So the ref called a penalty shootout to decide the game. Even though shooters have the advantage (see page 50), German goalkeeper Jens Lehmann didn't quake in his boots. Maybe that's because he was prepared. The coaching staff had shown Lehmann videos of all the penalty kicks taken by Argentina in the past two years. What's more, he stuffed a list of the way the Argentina players usually take penalty kicks in his sock. Lehmann studied the crumpled note between each kick and stopped two of the shooters cold. How's that for a "note-orious" victory!

Hand and Feet of a God?

Unstoppable, unequalled, and unapologetic. Diego Maradona was all three. The five-foot-five Argentinean midfielder could pounce on the ball like a tiger, find teammates with sharp passes, and dribble past a whole team with a blast to score.

Maradona could also do the unthinkable. During the 1986 World Cup, a defender lofted the ball back to England's goalkeeper Peter Shilton. The tall goalie leapt up for the ball and so did the short Argentinean. Maradona beat the keeper somehow and hammered the ball into the net with his hand. It happened so fast hardly anyone saw it and the ref signaled a goal. Later, TV replays revealed Maradona's illegal handiwork and he was unabashed. He said the "Hand of God" scored the goal.

Minutes later in the same game, Maradona scooped up the ball near midfield and tore toward the goal. He zoomed 60 yards in 10 seconds flat, dribbling circles around five defenders, and poked the ball into the net. After that, people said he had the feet of a god. And maybe he did for Maradona's unstoppable play led Argentina to victory at the 1986 World Cup.

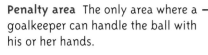

RULES AND REGS

THE FIELD

Soccer is played on a field shaped like a rectangle so play can flow between the target goals at each end.

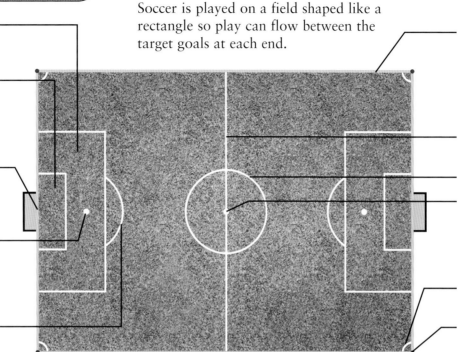

Penalty area The only area where a goalkeeper can handle the ball with his or her hands.

Goal area The area around the goal, inside the penalty area, that a goalie uses to tell where he or she is in relation to the goal during the game.

Goal line A goal is scored when the whole ball crosses this line between the goalposts and under the crossbar.

Penalty mark The spot where the ball is placed for a penalty kick; players other than the kicker must be behind this mark outside the penalty area until the ball is kicked.

Penalty arc During a penalty kick, all players expect the kicker and goalie must stand behind this arc.

Touchline When the whole ball crosses this line it is out of play; a throw-in by the team opposite to the last player who touched the ball restarts the game.

Halfway line Divides the field into halves.

Center circle

Center mark The spot where the team who has possession of the ball does the kickoff to start a game, a period, or play after a goal has been scored.

Corner arc Area where the ball is placed for a corner kick.

Corner flag Helps officials tell whether the ball has crossed the goal line or touchline.

THE PLAYERS

Defender A player who usually plays a defensive role in front of the goalkeeper.

Midfielder A player who usually plays in front of the defense and behind the attack, creating plays and scoring opportunities.

Forward A player who usually plays an attacking role.

Goalkeeper A player whose job is to keep the ball out of the net. A goalkeeper is the only player who may touch the ball with his or her hands.

Referee The top official of the game. The ref's job is to enforce the rules of the game.

Assistant Referees Two assistant referees help the referee enforce the rules. They indicate when players are offside, when players commit fouls, when the ball goes out of bounds or crosses the goal line, when a team gets a throw-in, penalty kick, corner kick, or the like.

HOW TO PLAY

• The object of the game is to score goals by putting the ball in the net.

• The team who scores the most goals wins.

• Each team may have no more than 11 players (usually a goalkeeper and a combination of defenders, midfielders, and forwards) on the field at once. In international or pro games, a team may have up to 3 substitutes.

• A match is played in two 45-minute periods, or halves. Players have a 15-minute break called halftime between halves.

• If the score is tied at the end of the second half, the game is a draw. If the match requires a winner, an extra period may be played. If it is still tied after that, a penalty kick shootout may be held to decide the winner.

Altitude — height of an object above sea level.

Assist — a pass that leads to a goal.

Assistant referee — an on-field official who helps the referee enforce the rules.

Attackers — players who go on the attack by trying to score goals.

Backheel — when a player strikes the ball with the back of his or her heel.

Banana kick — a kick that "bends the ball" (see below) so the ball's flight path curves like a banana.

Beautiful game — a term coined by the legendary player Pelé to describe soccer.

"Bend the ball" — when players kick the ball so it travels in a path that bends, or curves.

Bicycle Kick — when players kick the ball over their own head by doing a back flip and moving their feet through the air as if they were pedaling a bicycle.

Boots — a British term for soccer shoes.

Breakaway — when a player zooms in on goal without any opposing players between him or her and the goalkeeper.

Cap — each time players play an international match for their country they get credited with a cap. This credit comes from the tradition of giving players a knit cap for each game.

Catenaccio — "lock," or "great big chain," of defenders; a defensive formation developed by Italy.

Cleats — a term for soccer shoes, which also describes the studs attached to the sole of soccer shoes.

Coach — the person who manages the team during practices and games, sets team strategy, and chooses which players play.

Conditioning — physical training.

Corner Kick — the ref awards a corner kick to the attacking team when the defending team plays the ball over the goal line outside of the net.

Cross — passing the ball from either side of the field to the front of the opponent's goal.

Defenders — players whose main job is to help the goalkeeper guard the net and stymie attacking opponents.

Dribble — tapping the ball with and between the feet to move it up or down the field.

Elastico — pushing the ball one way with the outside of the foot then immediately bringing it back with the inside of the foot to foil defenders.

Extra time — an extra period of play held to decide the winner when the score is tied.

F. A. Cup — The Football Association Challenge Cup; the world-renowned knockout competition of English football that's the world's oldest football competition.

Fake — (also called juke) when a player with the ball gives a defender the slip by making it appear as if she or he is going to move in one direction and then moves in the other direction.

Far post — the goalpost farther away from the ball.

Field — the area of grass, or artificial turf, on which the game is played.

FIFA —Fédération Internationale de Football Association, the governing organization of world soccer, which runs all world championships, including the World Cup.

Fifty-fifty ball —a loose ball that either team can win.

Finisher — a goal scorer.

Formation — the way a team's players line up on the field at the beginning of a match. For example, a 4-4-2 formation is four defenders, four midfielders, and two forwards. The goalkeeper is not counted in the formation.

Forward — a player who usually plays an attacking role by trying to score or create goals.

Free Kick —interference-free kicks awarded to the opposing team when a player commits an offence, such as kicking, tripping, or charging an opponent; free kicks are direct or indirect; a direct kick can score; an indirect kick can score only if another player in addition to the kicker touches the ball before it enters the goal.

Goal — when a team scores by putting the ball in the net.

Goal Posts — one of two vertical posts that hold the crossbar of the net above the goal line.

Goal Kick — the ref awards the defending team a goal kick when the attacking team sends the ball over the goal line outside of the net; a player kicks the ball from anywhere inside the goal area and the attacking team must be outside the penalty area.

Hand ball — when a player, other than the goalkeeper, illegally strikes the ball with any part of his or her arm below the armpit.

Header — when a player strikes the ball with his or her head.

Instep Kick — when players kick the ball with the top of the foot between the ankle and the toes.

Libero — an Italian word for "free man"—a player behind the "chain of defenders" in Italy's *catenaccio* formation who can "close up" any breaks in the chain.

Man-to-man marking — a defense style in which players guard specific opponents all over the field.

Mental toughness — players' confidence and ability to handle the ups and downs of their performance and the game.

Midfield — the central part of the playing field.

Midfielder — a player who usually plays in front of the defense and behind the attack, creating plays and scoring opportunities.

Near post — the goalpost closest to the ball.

Nutmeg — dribble the ball between an opponent's legs and pick it up on the other side of the player.

Offside — when a player is closer to the opponent's goal line than both the ball and the second last opponent.

Outside Foot Kick — when players use the outside of the foot to kick the ball away quickly.

Own goal — when a player accidentally kicks, heads, or deflects the ball into his or her own goal; the score is credited to the opponents.

Pass — kicking or heading the ball to a teammate.

Penalty Kick — when a player commits an offence, such as kicking, tripping, or charging an opponent, inside his or her own penalty area, the ref awards the opponents a penalty kick; everyone except the kicker and goalkeeper must stay out of the penalty area until the ball is kicked.

Penalty Kick Shootout — when the score is tied and teams pick 5 players each to take penalty kicks to decide the winner of the game.

Pitch — a British term for a playing field.

Push Pass — when a player kicks the ball with the inside of the foot.

Red Card — when the referee throws a player out of the game for serious foul play or offences or repeated misconduct after receiving a "warning," or yellow card.

Referee — an on-field official who enforces the rules during the game.

Scissors — faking kicking the ball with the outside of the foot then stepping over the ball instead to foil defenders.

Set plays — (also called set pieces) plays, such as corner kicks and penalty kicks, that teams may set up to play during games.

Striker — a forward or attacker who tries to score and create goals.

Stoppage time — time the ref adds to the period of play to make up for the stops in the action due to injuries, fights, substitutions, and arguments from the bench.

Substitute — a player who replaces a teammate during the game.

Tackle — when players use their feet to try to take the ball from an opponent's feet.

Throw-in — when the ball goes over the touchline and an opponent of the last player who touched the ball throws the ball onto the field to restart the game.

Total Soccer — system played by the Dutch in which all team members play defense and offense, whirling from one to the other on the fly.

Touchline — a boundary line that encloses the playing field; when the whole ball goes over the line, the ball is out of play.

Transfer — when a player is sold from one team to another.

Trapping — when players stop a moving ball with their feet, legs, chest, or even their head.

UEFA — Union of European Football Associations; the governing body of soccer in Europe.

Visualization — imagining, or mentally rehearsing, moves, such as taking penalty kicks, so you can instinctively execute them successfully during games.

Wall — when defenders stand shoulder to shoulder in a row like a wall to create a barrier to stop the ball.

Winger — a player who usually plays on the wing, the right-hand or left-hand side of the field.

Work rate — a measure of how much players run and help their teams during a game.

World Cup — an international tournament, in which national teams from many different countries compete against each other, held every four years.

Zone defense — a defense style in which defenders stay in specific zones, or areas, and mark, or guard, all the players who enter the zone.

INDEX

Photo Credits

Answers

Try This page 17: Did you notice that the ball bounces higher on pavement than on grass? Pavement is a harder surface than grass, and it bounces the ball into the air with more energy than grass. When the ball bounces higher, it's harder for players to control. So chances are you'd rather play on grass than pavement.

Try This page 30: Chances are you'd rather play soccer in your sneakers than your thick winter boots. The softer and thinner the shoe, the easier it is to feel the ball with your feet. The more players can feel the ball like this, the better they can control the ball, dribble, and shoot on target to score.